BATTLEFIELD PRAYERS

PRAYER BOOK AND JOURNAL

Available online at:
barnesandnoble.com
amazon.com
christianbook.com
most online bookstores

Published by

WORD PRODUCTIONS

wordproductions.org • battlefieldprayers.com
Other prayer resources: prayerworkshop.com

Battlefield Prayers

PRAYER BOOK AND JOURNAL
©2006 by S. S. Parr
Published by Word Productions LLC

CAMOFLAGE: ISBN 0-9765010-0-7
DESERT: ISBN 0-9765010-2-3
BLUE: ISBN 0-9765010-1-5

Contents

Part I

Prayers 1

| **Chapter** | **Page** |

1. Revelation and Consecration 3

2. Prayer for the People
    of this Country 7

3. Guidance from the Holy Spirit.....................9

4. Divine Protection
    at All Times...17

5. God, Go with Us!
    Wisdom in Battle 25

6. David's Enemies
    Are Confused 31

7   Strategy:
    Wisdom and Knowledge 37

8. Provision
    for Our Needs 41

9. Heal the Injured
    and the Sick 45

Chapter	**Page**

10. Comfort and Heal
    Hearts and Minds 49
11. Comfort in Suffering:
    Peace of Mind and Heart........................53
12. Help for a Wounded
    Friend...57
13. Loss of Friend
    in Death...61

Part Two

Prayer Study...67
14. Spiritual Weapons:
    The Word of God in Prayer 69
15. The Power of Prayer:
    Kinds of Prayer..75
16. Prayer Workshop:
    Simple Steps..93
17. Prayer Promises
    to Rest Your Faith Upon 105

Part Three

Prayer Journal...115

Part One

Prayers

CHAPTER ONE

Revelation

AND CONSECRATION

Dear Father in heaven,
I present myself to You and I consecrate my life to
you. Thank You for sending Jesus Christ to die on
the cross for my sins and rise from the dead on the
third day. I accept Him as my Savior and Lord.
Jesus, come into my heart [spirit] by Your Holy
Spirit, right now. Be the Lord and Redeemer of my
life. Take control of my life, fill me with Your Holy
Spirit, and make me holy according to Your
sovereign plan. I ask You to reveal Yourself to me,
the truths of Jesus Christ the Son of God, and
what it means to me personally. I am trusting You,
the Creator of all things, to lead me into all truth.
I commit my life, spirit, soul, and body into Your
keeping, and I thank You for what You are going to
do in my life, in Jesus' name. Amen.

For God so loved the world that He gave His only begotten Son, that whoever believes in Him should not perish but have everlasting life. (John 3:16)

And this is eternal life, that they may know You, the only true God, and Jesus Christ whom You have sent. (John 17:3)

"For unto us a Child is born, unto us a Son is given; and the government will be upon His shoulder. And His name will be called Wonderful, Counselor, Mighty God, Everlasting Father, Prince of Peace." (Isaiah 9:6)

But of Him you are in Christ Jesus, who became for us wisdom from God—and righteousness and sanctification and redemption. (1 Corinthians 1:30)

Knowing that you were not redeemed with corruptible things, like silver or gold, from your aimless conduct received by tradition from your fathers, but with the precious blood of Christ, as of a lamb without blemish and without spot. (1 Peter 1:18, 19)

For even the Son of Man did not come to be served, but to serve, and to give His life a ransom for many. (Mark 10:45)

In whom we have redemption through His blood, the forgiveness of sins, according to the riches of His grace. (Ephesians 1:7)

When the fullness of the time was come, God sent forth His Son, made of a woman, made under the law, to redeem them that were under the law, that we might receive the adoption of sons. (Galatians 4:4, 5)

How much more shall the blood of Christ, Who through the eternal Spirit offered Himself without spot to God, purge your conscience from dead works to serve the living God? And for this cause He is the Mediator of the new testament, that by means of death, for the redemption of the transgressions that were under the first testament, they which are called might receive the promise of eternal inheritance. (Hebrews 9:14, 15)

Christ our passover is sacrificed for us. (1 Corinthians 5:7)

CHAPTER TWO

Prayer for the People
OF THIS COUNTRY

Dear heavenly Father,
I come to You in the name of Jesus, asking Your
blessing, love, and compassion on the people of
this country. Touch the lives of the men, women,
and children by Your Holy Spirit. Please provide for
their every need. Help us to do all we can to be a
blessing and help to this country in every possible
way. Heal any hurt or pain they may have
suffered. Touch their minds, hearts, and souls
according to Your divine will and purpose and
restore peace and comfort to each of them. Cause
all of us to have love and understanding for one
another and grant us peace in God. Help me and
my brothers and sisters to have a deep and
compassionate understanding for them, their
culture, and country, in Jesus' name.

"For the mountains shall depart and the hills be removed, but My kindness shall not depart from you, nor shall My covenant of peace be removed," says the Lord, who has mercy on you. (Isaiah 54:10)

Blessed be the Lord, for He has shown me His marvelous kindness in a strong city! (Psalm 31:21)

For His merciful kindness is great toward us, and the truth of the Lord endures forever. Praise the Lord! (Psalm 117:2)

Let, I pray, Your merciful kindness be for my comfort, according to Your word to Your servant. (Psalm 119:76)

Then they cried out to the Lord in their trouble, and He saved them out of their distresses. (Psalm 107:19)

CHAPTER THREE

Guidance
FROM THE HOLY SPIRIT

Dear God,
Guide my footsteps in Your Word and let no
iniquity have dominion over me. Lead me by Your
Holy Spirit. Enlighten my darkness. Cause me to
walk in the right path for Your name's sake. Lead
me in Your truth and teach me. Lord, You know
my path and You know the path of those who
fight against us. If necessary, redirect my steps in
Your wisdom. Grant those in authority Your
wisdom and guidance, Your knowledge for every
battle. Cause them to know the right strategy.
The Word says that if I ask anything according
to Your will You hear me and that I have the
petitions I ask of You. I thank You, in advance,
for what You are doing and are going to do, in
Jesus' name. Amen.

David Asks for God's Direction

It happened after this that David inquired
of the Lord, saying, "Shall I go up to any of
the cities of Judah?" And the Lord said to
him, "Go up." David said, "Where shall I
go up?" And He said, "To Hebron." So
David went up there, and his two wives
also, Ahinoam the Jezreelitess, and Abigail
the widow of Nabal the Carmelite. And
David brought up the men who were with
him, every man with his household. So
they dwelt in the cities of Hebron. Then
the men of Judah came, and there they
anointed David king over the house of
Judah. And they told David, saying, "The
men of Jabesh Gilead were the ones who
buried Saul." So David sent messengers to
the men of Jabesh Gilead, and said to
them, "You are blessed of the Lord, for you
have shown this kindness to your lord, to
Saul, and have buried him.

And now may the Lord show kindness and truth to you. I also will repay you this kindness, because you have done this thing. And now may the Lord show kindness and truth to you. I also will repay you this kindness, because you have done this thing. (2 Samuel 2:1-7)

Another King Seeks God's Direction
Now three years passed without war between Syria and Israel. Then it came to pass, in the third year, that Jehoshaphat the king of Judah went down to visit the king of Israel. And the king of Israel said to his servants, "Do you know that Ramoth in Gilead is ours, but we hesitate to take it out of the hand of the king of Syria?" So he said to Jehoshaphat, "Will you go with me to fight at Ramoth Gilead?" Jehoshaphat said to the king of Israel, "I am as you are, my people as your people, my horses as your horses."

Also Jehoshaphat said to the king of Israel, "Please inquire for the word of the Lord today." Then the king of Israel gathered the prophets together, about four hundred men, and said to them, "Shall I go against Ramoth Gilead to fight, or shall I refrain?" So they said, "Go up, for the Lord will deliver it into the hand of the king." And Jehoshaphat said, "Is there not still a prophet of the Lord here, that we may inquire of Him?" So the king of Israel said to Jehoshaphat, "There is still one man, Micaiah the son of Imlah, by whom we may inquire of the Lord; but I hate him, because he does not prophesy good concerning me, but evil." And Jehoshaphat said, "Let not the king say such things!" Then the king of Israel called an officer and said, "Bring Micaiah the son of Imlah quickly!" The king of Israel and Jehoshaphat the king of Judah, having put on their robes, sat each on his throne, at a threshing floor at the entrance of the gate of Samaria; and all the prophets prophesied before them. Now Zedekiah the son of Chenaanah had made horns of iron for himself; and he said, "Thus says the Lord: 'With these you shall gore the Syrians until they are destroyed.'" And all the prophets prophesied so, saying, "Go up to Ramoth Gilead and prosper, for the Lord will deliver it into the king's hand." Then the messenger who had gone to call Micaiah spoke to him, saying, "Now listen, the words of the prophets with one accord encourage the king. Please, let your word be like the word of one of them, and speak encouragement." And Micaiah said, "As the Lord lives, whatever the Lord says to me, that I will speak." (1 Kings 22: 1-14)

However, when He, the Spirit of truth, has come, He will guide you into all truth; for He will not speak on His own authority, but whatever He hears He will speak; and He will tell you things to come.
(John 16:13)

For this is God, our God forever and ever; He will be our guide even to death.
(Psalm 48:14)

You will guide me with Your counsel, and afterward receive me to glory.
(Psalm 73:24)

In all your ways acknowledge Him, and He shall direct your paths. (Proverbs 3:6)

A man's heart plans his way, but the Lord directs his steps. (Proverbs 16:9)

I will bring the blind by a way they did not know; I will lead them in paths they have not known. I will make darkness light before them, and crooked places straight. These things I will do for them, and not forsake them. (Isaiah 42:16)

Your ears shall hear a word behind you, saying, "This is the way, walk in it," whenever you turn to the right hand or whenever you turn to the left.
(Isaiah 30:21)

The Lord will guide you continually, and satisfy your soul in drought, and strengthen your bones; you shall be like a watered garden, and like a spring of water, whose waters do not fail. (Isaiah 58:11)

He restores my soul; He leads me in the paths of righteousness for His name's sake.
(Psalm 23:3)

They shall neither hunger nor thirst, neither heat nor sun shall strike them; for He Who has mercy on them will lead them, even by the springs of water He will guide them. (Isaiah 49:10)

CHAPTER FOUR

Divine Protection
AT ALL TIMES

Dear Heavenly Father,
I ask for Your divine protection for me, my brothers
and sisters, and for all You have entrusted in
my/our care. Send Your army of angels and
chariots of fire with us into battle. Protect me/us in
battle, in Jesus' name. You hold the heavens and
the earth in Your hands, and even if the earth were
removed and the mountains be cast into the sea,
I will not fear for You are with me. There is
nothing too hard for You. If I dwell in the secret
place of the Most High, I abide under the shadow
of the Almighty. Under Your shadow I take refuge.
Hide me in Your secret place. Hide us under the
shadow of Your wings. I commit myself/us to into
Your care, in Jesus' name. Amen.

God Signals David: More Guidance

Now when the Philistines heard that they had anointed David king over Israel, all the Philistines went up to search for David. And David heard of it and went down to the stronghold. The Philistines also went and deployed themselves in the Valley of Rephaim. So David inquired of the Lord, saying, "Shall I go up against the Philistines? Will You deliver them into my hand?" And the Lord said to David, "Go up, for I will doubtless deliver the Philistines into your hand." So David went to Baal Perazim, and David defeated them there; and he said, "The Lord has broken through my enemies before me, like a breakthrough of water." Therefore he called the name of that place Baal Perazim. And they left their images there, and David and his men carried them away. Then the Philistines went up once again and deployed themselves in the Valley of Rephaim. Therefore David inquired of the Lord, and He said, "You shall not go up; circle around behind them, and come upon them in front of the mulberry trees.

And it shall be, when you hear the sound of marching in the tops of the mulberry trees, then you shall advance quickly. For then the Lord will go out before you to strike the camp of the Philistines." And David did so, as the Lord commanded him; and he drove back the Philistines from Geba as far as Gezer.
(2 Samuel 5:17-25)

The Deep Sleep of the Lord

Then David answered, and said to Ahimelech the Hittite and to Abishai the son of Zeruiah, brother of Joab, saying, "Who will go down with me to Saul in the camp?" And Abishai said, "I will go down with you." So David and Abishai came to the people by night; and there Saul lay sleeping within the camp, with his spear stuck in the ground by his head. And Abner and the people lay all around him. Then Abishai said to David, "God has delivered your enemy into your hand this day. Now therefore, please, let me strike him at once with the spear, right to the earth; and I will not have to strike him a second time!" And David said to Abishai, "Do not destroy him; for who can stretch out his hand against the Lord's anointed, and be guiltless?" David said furthermore, "As the Lord lives, the Lord shall strike him, or his day shall come to die, or he shall go out to battle and perish. The Lord forbid that I should stretch out my hand against the Lord's anointed. But please, take now the spear and the jug of water that are by his head,

and let us go." So David took the spear
and the jug of water by Saul's head, and
they got away; and no man saw it or
knew it or awoke. For they were all
asleep, because a deep sleep from the
Lord had fallen on them.
(1 Samuel 26:6-12)

God Causes the Enemy to Fear

Now there were four leprous men at the
entrance of the gate; and they said to one
another, "Why are we sitting here until
we die? If we say, 'We will enter the city,'
the famine is in the city, and we shall die
there. And if we sit here, we die also.
Now therefore, come, let us surrender to
the army of the Syrians. If they keep us
alive, we shall live; and if they kill us, we
shall only die." And they rose at twilight
to go to the camp of the Syrians; and
when they had come to the outskirts of
the Syrian camp, to their surprise no one

was there. For the Lord had caused the army of the Syrians to hear the noise of chariots and the noise of horses—the noise of a great army; so they said to one another, "Look, the king of Israel has hired against us the kings of the Hittites and the kings of the Egyptians to attack us!" Therefore they arose and fled at twilight, and left the camp intact—their tents, their horses, and their donkeys—and they fled for their lives. And when these lepers came to the outskirts of the camp, they went into one tent and ate and drank, and carried from it silver and gold and clothing, and went and hid them; then they came back and entered another tent, and carried some from there also, and went and hid it. Then they said to one another, "We are not doing right. This day is a day of good news, and we remain silent. If we wait until morning light, some punishment will come upon us. Now therefore, come, let us go and tell the king's household." So they went and called to the gate-keepers of the city, and told them, saying, "We went to the Syrian camp, and surprisingly no one was there, not a human sound—only horses and donkeys tied, and the tents intact." And the gate-keepers called out, and they told it to the king's household inside. (2 Kings 7:3-11)

I will both lie down in peace, and sleep; For You alone, O Lord, make me dwell in safety. (Psalm 4:8)

He who dwells in the secret place of the Most High Shall abide under the shadow of the Almighty. I will say of the Lord, "He is my refuge and my fortress; My God, in Him I will trust." He shall cover you with His feathers, and under His wings you shall take refuge; His truth shall be your shield and buckler. No evil

shall befall you, nor shall any plague come near your dwelling.
(Psalm 91:1, 2, 4, 10)

But whoever listens to me will dwell safely, and will be secure, without fear of evil. (Proverbs 1:33)

CHAPTER FIVE

God, Go with Us!

WISDOM IN BATTLE

Lord God,
I thank You for all You have done for me, my
brothers and sisters, and for the men, women,
and children You have entrusted to our care.
I praise You for Your kindness and mercy for us.
You alone possess all power in heaven and in
earth, and there is nothing too hard for You. To
You belongs all might and power. I come to You
in Jesus' name, Father, and I ask You to
overthrow and overturn evil plans. Fight and
defeat them that fight against us. Let the net
which they have hidden catch them. Kings have
asked that You fight for them, drive their
enemies backward, and put them to shame and
confusion. You are fair and good to all who call
upon You. I ask help for us all, in Jesus' name.

And Asa cried out to the Lord his God, and said, "Lord, it is nothing for You to help, whether with many or with those who have no power; help us, O Lord our God, for we rest on You, and in Your name we go against this multitude.
O Lord, You are our God; do not let man prevail against You!" (2 Chronicles 14:11)

Then Jerubbaal (that is, Gideon) and all the people who were with him rose early and encamped beside the well of Harod, so that the camp of the Midianites was on the north side of them by the hill of Moreh in the valley And the Lord said to Gideon, "The people who are with you are too many for Me to give the Midianites into their hands, lest Israel claim glory for itself against Me, saying, 'My own hand has saved me.' Now therefore, proclaim in the hearing of the people, saying, 'Whoever is fearful and afraid, let him turn and depart at once from Mount Gilead.'" And twenty-two thousand of the people returned, and ten thousand remained. But the Lord said to Gideon, "The people are still too many; bring them down to the water, and I will test them for you there. Then it will be, that of whom I say to you, 'This one shall go with you,' the same shall go with you; and of whomever I say to you, 'This one shall not go with you,' the same shall not go." So he brought the people down to the water. And the Lord said to Gideon, "Everyone who laps from the water with his tongue, as a dog laps, you shall set apart by himself; likewise everyone who gets down on his knees to drink." And the number of those who lapped, putting their hand to their mouth, was three hundred men; but all the rest of the people got down on their knees to drink water. Then the Lord said to Gideon, "By the three hundred men who lapped I will save you, and deliver the Midianites into your hand. Let all the other people go, every man to his place." (Judges 7:1-7)

Many are the afflictions of the righteous, but the Lord delivers him out of them all. (Psalm 34:19)

Though I walk in the midst of trouble, You will revive me; You will stretch out Your hand against the wrath of my enemies, and Your right hand will save me. (Psalm 138:7)

Then they cried out to the Lord in their trouble, and He saved them out of their distresses. (Psalm 107:19)

Though he fall, he shall not be utterly cast down; For the Lord upholds him with His hand. But the salvation of the

righteous is from the Lord; He is their
strength in the time of trouble.
(Psalm 37:24, 39)

Indeed they shall surely assemble, but
not because of Me. Whoever assembles
against you shall fall for your sake. No
weapon formed against you shall prosper,
and every tongue which rises against you
in judgment you shall condemn. This is
the heritage of the servants of the Lord,
and their righteousness is from Me," says
the Lord. (Isaiah 54:15, 17)

The Lord will cause your enemies who
rise against you to be defeated before
your face; they shall come out against
you one way and flee before you seven
ways. (Deuteronomy 28:7)

For the Lord your God is He who goes with you, to fight for you against your enemies, to save you.
(Deuteronomy 20:4)

Through God we will do valiantly, for it is He who shall tread down our enemies.
(Psalm 60:12)

Do not be afraid of sudden terror, Nor of trouble from the wicked when it comes; For the Lord will be your confidence, and will keep your foot from being caught.
(Proverbs 3:25,26)

Behold, all those who were incensed against you shall be ashamed and disgraced; they shall be as nothing, and those who strive with you shall perish. You shall seek them and not find them—those who contended with you. Those who war against you shall be as nothing, as a nonexistent thing. (Isaiah 41:11,12)

CHAPTER SIX

David's Enemies

ARE CONFUSED

Dear heavenly Father,
I ask You, Father, to confuse our enemies in the name of Jesus. Grant us Your wisdom—not the wisdom of this world, but that which comes only from You. Bring to shame and confusion those that devise our hurt. Father, You have spoken to many. You have spoken to kings and can speak to anyone, according to Your will. Cause the enemy to be turned back. Foil their plans and strategies. Make seeing eyes blind. You know their plans and there is nothing that is hid from You. Let them fall into their own nets and traps. I thank You for Your manifest glory and I praise Your holy name, in Jesus' name. Amen.

Let those be put to shame and brought to dishonor Who seek after my life; let those be turned back and brought to confusion who plot my hurt. (Psalm 35:4)

God Speaks to People

Now there was a famine in the land, and Abram went down to Egypt to dwell there, for the famine was severe in the land. And it came to pass, when he was close to entering Egypt, that he said to Sarai his wife, "Indeed I know that you are a woman of beautiful countenance. Therefore it will happen, when the Egyptians see you, that they will say, 'This is his wife'; and they will kill me, but they will let you live. Please say you are my sister, that it may be well with me for your sake, and that I may live because of you." (Genesis 12:10-13)

Another time:

And Abraham journeyed from there to the South, and dwelt between Kadesh and Shur, and stayed in Gerar. Now Abraham said of Sarah his wife, "She is my sister." And Abimelech king of Gerar sent and took Sarah. But God came to Abimelech in a dream by night, and said to him, "Indeed you are a dead man because of the woman whom you have taken, for she is a man's wife." But Abimelech had not come near her; and he said, "Lord, will You slay a righteous nation also? Did he not say to me, 'She is my sister'? And she, even she herself said, 'He is my brother.' In the integrity of my heart and innocence of my hands I have done this." And God said to him in a dream, "Yes, I know that you did this in the integrity of your heart. For I also withheld you from sinning against Me; therefore I did not let you touch her.

Now therefore, restore the man's wife; for he is a prophet, and he will pray for you and you shall live. But if you do not restore her, know that you shall surely die, you and all who are yours.
(Genesis 20:1-7)

In my distress I called upon the Lord, and cried out to my God; He heard my voice from His temple, and my cry came before Him, even to His ears. Then the earth shook and trembled; the foundations of the hills also quaked and were shaken, because He was angry. Smoke went up from His nostrils, and devouring fire from His mouth; coals were kindled by it. He bowed the heavens also, and came down with darkness under His feet. And He rode upon a cherub, and flew; He flew upon the wings of the wind. He made darkness His secret place; His canopy around Him was dark waters and

thick clouds of the skies. From the brightness before Him, His thick clouds passed with hailstones and coals of fire. The Lord thundered from heaven, and the Most High uttered His voice, hailstones and coals of fire. He sent out His arrows and scattered the foe, lightnings in abundance, and He vanquished them.
(Psalm 18:6-4)

But if you go, be gone! Be strong in battle! Even so, God shall make you fall before the enemy; for God has power to help and to overthrow. (2 Chronicles 25:8)

CHAPTER SEVEN

Strategy

WISDOM AND KNOWLEDGE

Oh Lord God,
I praise You that nothing is hidden from You.
There is no one who knows what You know
unless You reveal it. Please grant us Your grace
and give us revelations, wisdom, and knowledge
by the Holy Spirit. Reveal plans of the enemy.
Grant knowledge and wisdom to come to the
minds of our intelligence. Reveal to me what I
need to know. Father, please turn, overthrow,
overturn, and cause us to escape every trap.
Guide our steps when we don't know which way
to go. We give You the glory and praise for all
You have done and for what You are going to do.
We ask these things based on Your promises in
the Word, and rely on You and Your power, and
give You all the glory, in Jesus' name. Amen.

God Revealed the Enemy's Plan

Now the king of Syria was making war against Israel; and he consulted with his servants, saying, "My camp will be in such and such a place." And the man of God sent to the king of Israel, saying, "Beware that you do not pass this place, for the Syrians are coming down there." Then the king of Israel sent someone to the place of which the man of God had told him. Thus he warned him, and he was watchful there, not just once or twice. Therefore the heart of the king of Syria was greatly troubled by this thing; and he called his servants and said to them, "Will you not show me which of us is for the king of Israel?" [he thought there was a spy in his camp.] And one of his servants said, "None, my lord, O king; but Elisha, the prophet, who is in Israel, tells the king of Israel the words that you speak in your bedroom." (2 Kings 6:8-12)

God Still Reveals Secrets

However, when He, the Spirit of truth, has come, He will guide you into all truth; for He will not speak on His own authority, but whatever He hears He will speak; and He will tell you things to come. (John 16:13)

Call to Me, and I will answer you, and show you great and mighty things, which you do not know. (Jeremiah 33:3)

At that time Jesus answered and said, "I thank You, Father, Lord of heaven and earth, that You have hidden these things from the wise and prudent and have revealed them to babes." (Matthew 11:25)

The secret of the Lord is with those who fear Him, and He will show them His covenant. (Psalm 24:14)

Therefore judge nothing before the time, until the Lord comes, Who will both bring to light the hidden things of darkness and reveal the counsels of the hearts. Then each one's praise will come from God. (I Corinthians 4:5)

Behold, You desire truth in the inward parts, and in the hidden part You will make me to know wisdom. (Psalm 51:6)

But God has revealed them to us through His Spirit. For the Spirit searches all things, yes, the deep things of God. (1 Corinthians 2:10)

The secret of the Lord is with those who fear Him, and He will show them His covenant. (Psalm 25:14)

CHAPTER EIGHT

Provision

FOR OUR NEEDS

Dear Heavenly Father,
I ask for You to provide for me and others
around me, in Jesus' name. Lord, to You do we
come for help. We need You, Lord, and we look
to You, in Jesus' name. We know that in the
Word, You have brought miraculous provision.
We believe You are limitless in power. You
provided manna in the desert when You led Your
children out of Egypt. Jesus fed a multitude with
a few loaves and fishes. You can provide for all.
I believe that You are true and Your Word is
true. Your Word says that You will provide for
all of our needs according to Your riches in glory
by Christ Jesus. I rest my faith in You, Your
integrity, and in the integrity of the Scriptures,
right now and I thank You for what You are
going to do, in Jesus' name. Amen.

~ Scriptural Confirmation ~

A Psalm of David. The Lord is my shepherd; I shall not want. You prepare a table before me in the presence of my enemies; You anoint my head with oil; my cup runs over. (Psalm 23:1, 5)

But seek first the kingdom of God and His righteousness, and all these things shall be added to you. (Matthew 6:33)

And my God shall supply all your need according to His riches in glory by Christ Jesus. (Philippians 4:19)

Trust in the Lord, and do good; dwell in the land, and feed on His faithfulness. (Psalm 37:3)

He has given food to those who fear Him; He will ever be mindful of His covenant. (Psalm 111:5)

He makes peace in your borders, and fills you with the finest wheat. (Psalm 147:14)

The righteous eats to the satisfying of his soul, but the stomach of the wicked shall be in want. (Proverbs 13:25)

Look at the birds of the air, for they neither sow nor reap nor gather into barns; yet your heavenly Father feeds them. Are you not of more value than they? (Matthew 6:26)

You shall eat in plenty and be satisfied, and praise the name of the Lord your God, Who has dealt wondrously with you; And My people shall never be put to shame. (Joel 2:26)

Therefore I say to you, do not worry about your life, what you will eat or what you will drink; nor about your body, what you will put on. Is not life more than food and the body more than clothing? Now if God so clothes the grass of the field, which today is, and tomorrow is thrown into the oven, will He not much more clothe you, O you of little faith? Therefore do not worry, saying, "What shall we eat?" or "What shall we drink?" or "What shall we wear?" For after all these things the Gentiles seek. For your heavenly Father knows that you need all these things. (Matthew 6:25, 30, 31, 32)

CHAPTER NINE

Heal the Injured

AND THE SICK

Dear God,
I ask that You consider the needs of the sick and
injured. Please breathe Your breath of life into me,
and my suffering friend. You heal the sick and
raise the dead. Miracles exist today. You are a
present help in the time of trouble. Father, grant
healing and cause the healing power of Jesus to fill
my/their body, mind, soul, and spirit. You are
Jehovah Rapha [the Lord that heals] and I ask for
healing in Jesus' name. Thank You, God, that You
are limitless in power and might. Thank You for
touching me and my friend by Your Spirit, right
now. I thank You that You are true and Your Word
is true. I rest my faith on You, Your power, and on
Your Word and promises. Thank You for what You
are going to do, in Jesus' name. Amen.

Who forgives all your iniquities, Who
heals all your diseases, Who redeems
your life from destruction, Who crowns
you with lovingkindness and tender
mercies, Who satisfies your mouth with
good things, and that your youth is
renewed like the eagle's. (Psalm 103:3-5)

He sent His word and healed them, and
delivered them from their destructions.
(Psalm 107:20)

For they are life to those who find them,
and health to all their flesh.
(Proverbs 4:22)

So you shall serve the Lord your God,
and He will bless your bread and your
water. And I will take sickness away from
the midst of you. (Exodus 23:25)

...If you diligently heed the voice of the Lord your God and do what is right in His sight, give ear to His commandments and keep all His statutes, I will put none of the diseases on you which I have brought on the Egyptians. For I am the Lord who heals you. (Exodus 15:26)

Behold, I will bring it health and healing; I will heal them and reveal to them the abundance of peace and truth. (Jeremiah 33:6)

...And Peter said to him, "Aeneas, Jesus the Christ heals you. Arise and make your bed." And he arose immediately. And when He had called His twelve disciples to Him, He gave them power over unclean spirits, to cast them out, and to heal all kinds of sickness and all kinds of disease. (Matthew 10:1)

Heal the sick, cleanse the lepers, raise the dead, cast out demons. Freely you have received, freely give. (Matthew 10:8)

The Spirit of the Lord is upon Me, because He has anointed Me to preach the gospel to the poor; He has sent Me to heal the brokenhearted, to preach deliverance to the captives and recovery of sight to the blind, to set at liberty those who are oppressed. (Luke 4:18)

CHAPTER TEN

Comfort and Heal

HEARTS AND MINDS

Heavenly Father,
I can't handle this situation. Touch my mind by
Your Holy Spirit, Father, in Jesus' name. I give
my mind and emotions to You, right now. Please
heal and comfort my mind and heart and soul.
Hold me up above these things I am exper-
iencing, as I cannot handle them in my own
strength. The Scriptures tell us to cast our cares
totally on You and to trust in You for every need.
I turn all of this pain and turmoil over to You
totally right now, and I am going to trust in
Your help for all of this. I commit all of this to
You right now. Grant supernatural peace by Your
Holy Spirit, in Jesus' name. I rest my faith in
Your promises. I will now thank You in faith for
what You are doing.

By this I know that You are well pleased with me, because my enemy does not triumph over me. (Psalm 41:11)

Then they cried out to the Lord in their trouble, and He saved them out of their distresses. (Psalm 107:19)

The righteous is delivered from trouble, and it comes to the wicked instead. (Proverbs 11:8)

The wicked is ensnared by the transgression of his lips, but the righteous will come through trouble. (Proverbs 12:13)

For I know the thoughts that I think toward you, says the Lord, thoughts of peace and not of evil, to give you a future and a hope. (Jeremiah 29:11)

Therefore they shall come and sing in the height of Zion, streaming to the goodness of the Lord— for wheat and new wine and oil, for the young of the flock and the herd; their souls shall be like a well-watered garden, and they shall sorrow no more at all. Then shall the virgin rejoice in the dance, and the young men and the old, together; for I will turn their mourning to joy, will comfort them, and make them rejoice rather than sorrow. (Jeremiah 31:12, 13)

The Lord also will be a refuge for the oppressed, a refuge in times of trouble. (Psalm 9:9)

For He has not despised nor abhorred the affliction of the afflicted; nor has He hidden His face from Him; but when He cried to Him, He heard. (Psalm 22:24)

Wait on the Lord; be of good courage, and He shall strengthen your heart; wait, I say, on the Lord! (Psalm 27:10, 14)

To the Chief Musician. A Psalm of the sons of Korah. A Song for Alamoth. God is our refuge and strength, a very present help in trouble. Therefore we will not fear, even though the earth be removed, and though the mountains be carried into the midst of the sea; though its waters roar and be troubled, though the mountains shake with its swelling. Selah. (Psalm 46:1-3)

O Lord, my strength and my fortress, my refuge in the day of affliction, the Gentiles shall come to You from the ends of the earth and say, "Surely our fathers have inherited lies, worthlessness and unprofitable things. (Jeremiah 16:19)

CHAPTER ELEVEN

Comfort in Suffering

PEACE OF MIND AND HEART

Dear Lord God,
Hold me up above these circumstances, Lord. I
ask You to hide me under the shadow of Your
wings and in Your high tower. You are El
Shaddai, the All-sufficient One. Father, Your
Word tells those who suffer to commit them-
selves and their souls to You. Even Jesus from the
cross committed His spirit into Your hands. I
right now place my spirit, soul, mind, and body
into Your hands. You alone are God. You alone
can heal me. You are the resurrection and the
Life. If any man believe in You, Jesus, though He
were dead yet shall he live...and any man that
lives and believes in You shall never die. I trust
You to be my healer, comforter, and strength,
and ask for it in Jesus' name. Thank You for
what You are going to do.

I will give peace in the land, and you shall lie down, and none will make you afraid; I will rid the land of evil beasts, and the sword will not go through your land. (Leviticus 26:6)

The Lord will give strength to His people; the Lord will bless His people with peace. (Psalm 29:11)

Great peace have those who love Your law, and nothing causes them to stumble. (Psalm 119:165)

Behold, God is my salvation, I will trust and not be afraid; for Yah, the Lord, is my strength and song; He also has become my salvation. (Isaiah 12:2)

He gives power to the weak, and to those who have no might He increases strength. Even the youths shall faint and be weary, and the young men shall utterly fall, but those who wait on the Lord shall renew their strength; they shall mount up with wings like eagles, they shall run and not be weary, they shall walk and not faint. (Isaiah 40:29-31)

And He said to me, "My grace is sufficient for you, for My strength is made perfect in weakness." Therefore most gladly I will rather boast in my infirmities, that the power of Christ may rest upon me. (2 Corinthians 12:9)

Be of good courage, and He shall strengthen your heart, all you who hope in the Lord. (Psalm 31:24)

O God, You are more awesome than Your holy places. The God of Israel is He who gives strength and power to His people. Blessed be God! (Psalm 68:35)

Strengthen the weak hands, and make firm the feeble knees. Say to those who are fearful-hearted, "Be strong, do not fear! Behold, your God will come with vengeance, With the recompense of God; He will come and save you."
(Isaiah 35:3, 4)

But the Lord will be a shelter for His people, and the strength of the children of Israel. (Joel 3:16)

For God has not given us a spirit of fear, but of power and of love and of a sound mind. (2 Timothy 1:7)

CHAPTER TWELVE

Help for a Wounded

FRIEND

Lord Jesus,
Why did this happen to my friend and not me?
Please heal my heart and remove all sorrow and
condemnation from me. You are able to remove
these guilty feelings from me. Rather, direct my
feelings toward compassion and prayer for
others, and for the men, women, and children
who are in need around me. Although I do not
understand what is going on fully, I know You
know all things, and I commit it all into Your
hands. I also commit to You the body, mind,
soul, and spirit of my friend. Let Your healing
power and life fill his/her body in Jesus' name.
Let Your glory be seen. Surround us all with Your
grace. Thank You, for Your help, kindness, and
tender mercies toward us.

So we may boldly say: "The Lord is my helper; I will not fear. What can man do to me?" (Hebrews 13:6)

The Lord is on my side; I will not fear. What can man do to me? (Psalm 118:6)

So you shall serve the Lord your God, and He will bless your bread and your water. And I will take sickness away from the midst of you. (Exodus 23:25)

"...If you diligently heed the voice of the Lord your God and do what is right in His sight, give ear to His commandments and keep all His statutes, I will put none of the diseases on you which I have brought on the Egyptians. For I am the Lord who heals you." (Exodus 15:26)

He who dwells in the secret place of the Most High shall abide under the shadow of the Almighty. I will say of the Lord,

"He is my refuge and my fortress; my God, in Him I will trust." Surely He shall deliver you from the snare of the fowler and from the perilous pestilence. He shall cover you with His feathers, and under His wings you shall take refuge; His truth shall be your shield and buckler. You shall not be afraid of the terror by night, nor of the arrow that flies by day, nor of the pestilence that walks in darkness, nor of the destruction that lays waste at noonday. A thousand may fall at your side, and ten thousand at your right hand; but it shall not come near you. Only with your eyes shall you look, and see the reward of the wicked. Because you have made the Lord, who is my refuge, even the Most High, your dwelling place, no evil shall befall you, nor shall any plague come near your dwelling; for He shall give His angels charge over you, to keep you in all your ways.

(Psalm 91:1-11)

Who forgives all your iniquities, Who heals all your diseases. (Psalm 103:3)

The Lord will strengthen him on his bed of illness; You will sustain him on his sickbed. (Psalm 41:3)

"Then shall the virgin rejoice in the dance, And the young men and the old, together; for I will turn their mourning to joy, will comfort them, and make them rejoice rather than sorrow." (Jeremiah 31:13).

CHAPTER THIRTEEN

Loss of Friend

IN DEATH

Dear God,
Please comfort the hearts of my friend's family.
Hold them up above their pain and in Your
heavenly peace. My heart is also broken. Send
Your Holy Spirit to comfort. Thank You for being
with each one who is near to death. Please grant
us the grace to remember that death is merely a
temporary separation. We shall all be together
for eternity with You, through salvation in Jesus
Christ. Grant us the mercy and grace to go on
and to live in Your grace. I ask all of these things
in Jesus' name. Grant Your special grace and
preparation for all those who are appointed to
die. I am thankful for Your compassion and
kindness. I thank You for what You are doing, in
Jesus' name. Amen.

But God will redeem my soul from the power of the grave, for He shall receive me. Selah. (Psalm 49:15)

For this is God, Our God forever and ever; He will be our guide even to death. (Psalm 48:14)

My flesh and my heart fail; but God is the strength of my heart and my portion forever. (Psalm 73:26)

For I am persuaded that neither death nor life, nor angels nor principalities nor powers, nor things present nor things to come, nor height nor depth, nor any other created thing, shall be able to separate us from the love of God which is in Christ Jesus our Lord. (Romans 8:38, 39)

He will swallow up death forever, and the Lord God will wipe away tears from all faces; the rebuke of His people He will take away from all the earth; for the Lord has spoken. (Isaiah 25:8)

Therefore we do not lose heart. Even though our outward man is perishing, yet the inward man is being renewed day by day. (2 Corinthians 4:16)

Yea, though I walk through the valley of the shadow of death, I will fear no evil; for You are with me; Your rod and Your staff, they comfort me. (Psalm 23:4)

"I will ransom them from the power of the grave; I will redeem them from death. O Death, I will be your plagues! O Grave, I will be your destruction! Pity is hidden from My eyes." (Hosea 13:14)

O Death, where is your sting? O Hades, where is your victory? But thanks be to God, who gives us the victory through our Lord Jesus Christ.
(1 Corinthians 15:55, 57)

For in the time of trouble He shall hide me in His pavilion; in the secret place of His tabernacle He shall hide me; He shall set me high upon a rock. And now my head shall be lifted up above my enemies all around me; therefore I will offer sacrifices of joy in His tabernacle; I will sing, yes, I will sing praises to the Lord.
(Psalm 27:5, 6)

So he answered, "Do not fear, for those who are with us are more than those who are with them." (2 Kings 6:16)

"I know the thoughts that I think toward you," saith the LORD, "thoughts of peace, and not of evil, to give you an expected end." (Jeremiah 29:11)

He heals the broken hearted, and binds up their wounds. (Psalm 147:3)

Now the Lord of peace himself give you peace always by all means.
(2 Thessalonians 3:16)

He shall give his angels charge over you, to keep you in all your ways. They shall bear you up in their hands, lest you dash your foot against a stone.
(Psalm 91:11, 12)

Let the peace of God rule in your hearts, to which also you were called in one body, and be thankful. (Colossians 3:15)

Peace I leave with you, My peace I give to you: not as the world gives do I give to you. (John 14:27)

Part Two

Prayer Study

CHAPTER FOURTEEN

Spiritual Weapons

THE WORD OF GOD IN PRAYER

The next few chapters contain teaching contained in *The Prayer Workshop*.

Spiritual warfare is accomplished when we take everything to God. Ephesians 6:18 says, "praying always with all prayer and supplication in the Spirit..." This says it all.

What does "all prayer"include? It includes thanksgiving, praise, worship, prayer in the Spirit, supplication, and standing on specific promises [the Amplified Bible describes it as resting the whole of our confidence and trust on God].

Unless God specifically leads you to address the devil, don't. Keep your focus on Him and on what He has called you to do.

Ask God to fight your spiritual battles in Jesus' name and trust in His power.

For we do not wrestle against flesh and blood, but against principalities, against powers, against the rulers of the darkness of this age, against spiritual hosts of wickedness in the heavenly places. Ephesians 6:12

In this life we aren't playing games. There is a very real battle going on. His Word is a spiritual weapon. In the book of Ephesians, when Paul is teaching the Body of Christ about their armor, he says:

And take the helmet of salvation, and the sword of the Spirit which is the Word of God; praying always with all prayer and supplication in the Spirit, being watchful to this end with all perseverance and supplication for all the saints. Ephesians 6:17–18

For the Word of God is living and powerful, and sharper than any two-edged sword, piercing even to the division of soul and spirit, and of joints and marrow, and is a discerner of the thoughts and intents of the heart.
Hebrews 4:12

Learn To Use the Sword

Learn to apply and use the Word of God properly. It is like the difference between children who play at sword fighting and a swordsman who, after much training, has developed his skill. He is a master at what he does. The muscles he uses have become developed and strong. He has become quick, and when he strikes with the sword, he hits his target forcefully. It didn't come overnight, but now, after much training we become master swordsmen with the Word of God! Jesus stood on Scripture when He faced temptation (Matthew 4). The very Word of

God proceeded from His mouth. The Word of God is the sword of the Spirit. Remember this vital part of Scripture: "praying always with all prayer and supplication in the Spirit" (Eph. 6:18). Praying in the Spirit is a supernatural weapon.

There is supernatural power in the Word of God. It is spiritual food, and it is the sword of the Spirit. The enemy must flee at the name of Jesus, and God's Word is a weapon.

> *Having disarmed principalities and powers, He made a public spectacle of them, triumphing over them in it.*
> Colossians 2:15

One example of prayer using the Sword of the Spirit follows:

> *Father Your Word says in Psalm 27 that You are the strength of my life. I thank You for it! You are no respecter of*

persons Your Word says that You are
able to do more than I can ask or even
think. There is nothing too hard for
You. You are the Mighty God, limitless
in power. Your Word will not return
void! I praise You for what You are
doing in my life (or in the life of the
person for whom you are praying).

Can you find the Scripture within the above prayer? There are seven Scriptures mentioned in this prayer. Jesus has already defeated Satan for you through His redemptive work of the cross. We make this living reality through prayer and by the appropriation of God's Word and promises for our own lives (2 Corinthians 10:4; 1 Peter 5:9).

CHAPTER FIFTEEN

The Power of Prayer

KINDS OF PRAYER

Some of the most important Scriptures and secrets I can share with you are in this chapter. God is alive now. Finding that out will change your life forever. Knowing how great and powerful He is, and reading the following reminders will refresh you and bring it alive again.

2 Chronicles 20:12–22 tells the story of the prophet Johaz. The Spirit of the Lord told him to tell the people not be afraid of the great multitude that was coming against them. It was the Lord's battle and not theirs. When they began to sing and to praise, the Lord caused an ambush against their enemies. This is an exciting example of what

God can do when we look to Him, worship
Him, and praise Him! Read the Scripture:

"O our God, will You not judge them?
For we have no power against this great
multitude that is coming against us;
nor do we know what to do, but our
eyes are upon You." Now all Judah,
with their little ones, their wives, and
their children, stood before the Lord.
Then the Spirit of the Lord *came upon*
Jahaziel the son of Zechariah, the son
of Benaiah, the son of Jeiel, the son of
Mattaniah, a Levite of the sons of
Asaph, in the midst of the assembly.
And he said, "Listen, all you of Judah
and you inhabitants of Jerusalem, and
you, King Jehoshaphat! Thus says the
Lord *to you: 'Do not be afraid nor dis-*
mayed because of this great multitude,
for the battle is not yours, but God's.
Tomorrow go down against them. They

will surely come up by the Ascent of Ziz, and you will find them at the end of the brook before the Wilderness of Jeruel. You will not need to fight in this battle. Position yourselves, stand still and see the salvation of the LORD, who is with you, O Judah and Jerusalem!' Do not fear or be dismayed; tomorrow go out against them, for the LORD is with you." And Jehoshaphat bowed his head with his face to the ground, and all Judah and the inhabitants of Jerusalem bowed before the LORD, worshiping the LORD. Then the Levites of the children of the Kohathites and of the children of the Korahites stood up to praise the LORD God of Israel with voices loud and high. So they rose early in the morning and went out into the Wilderness of Tekoa; and as they went out, Jehoshaphat stood and said, "Hear me, O Judah and you inhabitants of

Jerusalem: Believe in the LORD your God, and you shall be established; believe His prophets, and you shall prosper." And when he had consulted with the people, he appointed those who should sing to the LORD, and who should praise the beauty of holiness, as they went out before the army and were saying: "Praise the LORD, For His mercy endures forever." Now when they began to sing and to praise, the LORD set ambushes against the people of Ammon, Moab, and Mount Seir, who had come against Judah; and they were defeated. 2 Chronicles 20:12–22

Prayer of the Spirit

When we pray in the Spirit, the Holy Spirit takes over, praying through us according to God's will. The following Scriptures mention this kind of prayer:

Likewise the Spirit also helps in our weaknesses. For we do not know what we should pray for as we ought, but the Spirit Himself makes intercession for us with groanings which cannot be uttered. Romans 8:26

But you, beloved, building yourselves up on your most holy faith, praying in the Holy Spirit... Jude 20

Waiting in the Presence of God

I have found "waiting in the presence of God" to be an extremely effective type of prayer that always brings huge results.

While attending Bible college, I had a remarkable experience that I want to share with you. This experience will help you to understand what this type of prayer can do.

One of my teachers was an intercessor. During one of his classes he shared a valuable insight with the class. He told us that the most powerful and greatest kind of prayer was waiting in the presence of God on behalf of someone or some situation. He said he didn't know why it was so powerful, but that his experience had proven it to be so. I just listened and wondered about it.

"Mom" Goodwin

I left class that day to drive to Mom Goodwin's house. "Mama," as I called her, was my spiritual mother. She was living in Broken Arrow, Oklahoma at the time. She had moved there after her husband went home to be with the Lord. She and her husband, Rev. J. R. Goodwin, were pastors for forty-eight years in the Assemblies of God churches and were written about in John Sherril's book *They Speak with Other Tongues*. They knew about the moving of the Holy Spirit.

Mom had a ministry of intercession. She would have an experience, dream, or word of knowledge...then pray about it. In the next few days she would see what she prayed about on the news or in the lives of those they ministered to. They were known for their counseling ministry to ministers.

Frequently, I went to her house to fix her hair, clean her house, cook a meal, or for fellowship and prayer. We spent many hours together. My association with Mom Goodwin was a special blessing to my life. I will use fictional names for my other friends in the story.

I continued driving to her house and twice these thoughts came to mind: "Jennie and John [fictional names] can't get out of the Middle East. If someone would wait in God's presence on their behalf, God could get them out of the country." Mind you, I didn't know they couldn't get out of Jordan.

I pulled into the driveway, got out of the car, and walked up to the door where Mom Goodwin met me. Before I even stepped inside, she said these words, "I just got a call from Voralee (I used to rent from her while in Bible school), and she got a letter from Jennie and they say they can't get out of the Middle East."

I said, "Mom, you won't believe what just happened while driving over here." I told her about the Bible teaching on prayer, and about the thoughts that came to me on my way to her house.

"That sounds like God to me. You better do it."

I was excited. That night I sat in the presence of God on their behalf. I had sought the Lord many times, but this time I just sat there feeling foolish thinking: *You are the mighty God...I am nothing.* I wondered, *Should I read a Scripture? Do I do anything?* I pretty much just sat there in the presence of God, remembering part of Brother Lawrence's book *The Practice of the Presence of God: With Spiritual Maxims.* But I didn't feel anything.

In two days I got word that my friends

gained legal permission to leave the Middle East. Others had been praying. There was one particular guy who told me he was praying every day "in the Spirit" for them. God moved when I waited in His presence. While I'm sure God uses many people and many prayers, in this instance, the test for whether it was of God, is whether or not what God says comes to pass. This was really God's Spirit speaking to me. Everything God said would happen came to pass when I prayed as He directed me to pray.

The Next Year

Almost a year to the date, Jennie and John told me that John's brother couldn't get out of the Middle East. He wanted to come to the United States to go to school, but had been turned down eleven times by Europe and the U.S.

The next morning I had a dream before waking: I felt an intense love in my heart.

Then I heard myself speaking to John, "John, I will pray. God can get your brother out of the country." I awoke with that.

"What will John think if I tell him that? What if that wasn't the Lord?" I thought about it for quite awhile with mixed feelings of excitement, wonder, and concern. I knew that God could do this. The experience was mixed with a tremendous amount of love and the knowledge that God had done it for my friends a year earlier. I decided that I would be careful how I said it, but that I would go and tell them that night.

"John," I began, "I'll pray. God can get your brother out of the country."

"Oh, thank you," he said.

That was it! I went home and did it.

I guess I spent about an hour waiting in God's presence. I also spent some time the next day, hoping to feel like I was done waiting in His presence for the need. In two days, permission was granted for my friend's brother to come to the U.S.

Through this kind of prayer God moves mountains; binds devils; overthrows the powers of darkness; sends His mighty; heavenly armies; and subdues the enemy in the situation. I don't know why it is so powerful. Maybe part of it is spending that time with Him. He is high and lifted up; you are the helpless one coming to Him. When all hope seems gone and you don't know what to do, wait in God's presence on behalf of the situation.

Miracles in Spain

More recently, my youngest son decided to take a trip to Spain with just his backpack to "live off the land." He went through many situations. I prayed all the way through it and there were many day-to-day miracles. Just before he came back this country, some interesting events took place. Here is the condensed version:

Two mornings in a row I woke around 4 AM and felt led by the Holy Spirit to wait in God's presence on his behalf.

Each day, there were specific things I felt I should share with my son.

The first morning I felt led to tell my son about an experience I had at about his age. God caused deep feelings within me that I should not go a certain direction. I had a horrible feeling inside me about taking that direction. For almost a month those intense feelings came and went.

I never experienced anything like that and didn't know what to make of it. I couldn't figure it out. I didn't listen to the "don't do it" feelings, and I followed what I thought, instead of my heart.

I ended up in a bad situation. Because of all that transpired, I realized that God Himself had spoken to me.

I told my son about the experience, and told him that this was the first time God spoke to me that way, I didn't even realize that God could do such at thing, although I loved God and cared about God in my life.

I wished I had known it was God.

After sharing it with my son, I had to tell him that I would trust his wisdom and just asked him to be sensitive to his gut feelings.

The next morning I woke with the knowledge that I was to pray, and here's what happened: Shortly after I began praying, I felt like I should call my son. If I hadn't called him right at that moment I would have missed him. He was on a train headed toward France. He said:

"I just wanted to tell you that it happened to me...I felt inside of me that I should come home. But I want to test it. Nothing like this has ever happened to me."

I thought *Oh no...if God wants him home and he's headed toward France, now what?* I was concerned that he might be headed for trouble.

Soon he was out of cell phone reach. I called a few of prayer partners and asked them to pray, and I went on to work.

The next morning I felt like I should try and call him one more time. I thought, "Perhaps he is now in an area where he can be reached by cell phone."

Here is what I found out happened after he had last talked to me: He had gotten off the train in France and found somewhere to sleep for the night. *Waking, a feeling came over him that he couldn't do this anymore, that he was drained, and that this was the end of him trying to 'live off the land' in Europe.*

I later knew that this was God's voice speaking to him. God had spoken to my son, even though he wasn't sure it was God speaking.

He got on a plane and came back to Madrid, where he was getting ready to board a plane to New York! Thank God he had left money in the bank for a trip home.

The moment I called him, he was indeed in calling range (his cell phone was only for Spain).

"I'm so glad you called me", he said. "I was hoping you would. I'm getting on a plane for the United States right now. In fact, if you had waited a minute, we would be taking off and you couldn't have gotten through to me."

My son got on the plane and was soon back at work in the states. Since that time, my son has had a beautiful revelation of the reality of Christ. God keeps proving himself to him! His adventures have only begun!

God's Power Displayed

While finishing up this book, a beautiful example of waiting in God's presence took place.

It was four in the morning and I couldn't sleep. I am an early morning person anyway. I went downstairs, ready to have devotions, when the phone rang. It was a friend of mine calling from Michigan. "Jimmy is on life support. He's brain dead and on a respirator. They're going stop using the respirator at eleven this morning."

I couldn't believe it! This is a young man our prayer group had been praying for. His father said that he had been experiencing sleep apnea, and that he just stopped breathing. I told him that I had gotten up to pray and would pray. I made a couple of calls to prayer partners and began to wait in God's presence. It is two hours earlier where I was.

Around six, I felt something although I didn't know what it meant and just remained before the Lord. I prayed a few things as I waited, such as that God would send his angels to the hospital in Michigan, pour out His Spirit, and that if He could minister to

Jimmy in his condition, that He would. I asked God, that if he could speak to him even if in a coma, that He would. "Have mercy on him Lord. Remember him as a child. I ask for your kindness toward him. You are the only One that can help him. Please don't let him die without being ready."

Those prayers, are basically all I could think of to pray.

At 8:10, the Scripture came to me, "I am the resurrection and the life. He who believes in Me, though he may die, he shall live. And whoever lives and believes in Me shall never die..." (John 11:25–26).

I thought... *"that's nice, I love that Scripture."* I didn't realize what was happening. I felt strongly that God wanted me to stay before Him for Jimmy.

Then, from 8:15 to 8:30 the most wonderful thing I've ever experienced happened to me. God poured out His powerful, supernatural presence on me. I was filled with gratitude and worship. I praised Him with a supernatural awareness of His goodness, kindness, compassion. "How wonderful God was to Jimmy. God was Almighty. He was Great!"

Jesus had filled my being with true worship...I wept for joy. I had joy I had never before experienced in my Spirit. It was great. I *knew* Jimmy was okay. There were now only thirty minutes left before the hospital was going to remove the respirator.

I decided I should stay before the Lord until that time. At eleven Michigan time, a tremendous silent presence of God came over me. I just felt like a child. I thought *"Maybe Jesus and His angels are ready to take Jimmy."*

He was. As the respirator was removed from Jimmy, his dad holding his hand, Jimmy left this life...but stepped into glory with the Lord Jesus.

CHAPTER SIXTEEN

Prayer Workshop

SIMPLE STEPS

This next chapter will give you the step-by-step method found in *The Prayer Workshop*. In it, you will find out the keys to results in prayer. It's not a matter of using a key to "get want you want" as though there is any selfishness involved. There is no selfishness whatsoever in the following method. I use the word "key" because I found, to my joy, that making a few changes in how I was praying totally regenerated my prayer life and filled my heart and mind with peace.

> *Be anxious for nothing, but in every-*
> *thing by prayer and supplication, with*
> *thanksgiving, let your requests be made*
> *known to God; and the peace of God,*

which surpasses all understanding, will guard your hearts and minds through Christ Jesus. Philippians 4:6–7

The above verse is the theme Scripture for *The Prayer Workshop*. This bit of advice from the apostle Paul sums it up: Don't worry, instead, pray about everything. It then adds that the peace of God, which surpasses understanding, will keep our hearts and minds through Christ Jesus. What a promise! Of course, we must pray according to God's will and in line with what Scripture teaches us. But many things *are* God's will.

In the Old Testament, David prayed that God would overthrow and overturn the works of darkness, and in response God sent out His arrows and scattered the foe, lightnings in abundance, and He vanquished them (Psalm 18:14). There are many answers to personal prayers in the Bible. Have you ever wanted to pray but didn't know how to begin? Or have you tried everything but not received the joy and fulfillment you had hoped for in prayer?

Through these steps, you will become renewed in your excitement for spiritual things and about God Himself, His faithfulness, and the integrity of His Word. If you already have received answers, you will be further inspired and become even more full of faith in God. Through spending time with God in prayer, you will experience the priceless treasure of developing a relationship with God.

The price Jesus paid for our sins at Calvary affords us the opportunity to be born again and to come into the family of God, which is the Christian's greatest gift. The relationship we can then have with our God is the next greatest gift.

Prayer is the key to building a close relationship with God. As you engage in prayer, you will never be the same again.

Prayer need not be tedious. God does not require you to perform a list of prerequisites before He will answer you. Yet there are things that God asks of us.

Before You Start: Forgiveness

Before you pray, you need to be sure there is nothing between you and God. You need to ask for forgiveness of your sins. You also need to forgive others of anything you have against them. How can we ask for forgiveness if we refuse to forgive others their trespasses against us (Luke 6:37 and 17:3)? If I feel like I can't forgive, I ask for His help: "God, I can't forgive, but I ask You to love and forgive in and through me by Your Holy Spirit. Please give me the grace." This will work!

> *Leave your gift there before the altar, and go your way. First be reconciled to your brother, and then come and offer your gift.* Matthew 5:24

Enemies to Answered Prayer

Look at the list of hindrances to prayer below. Take time to pray about these issues in your life. Once you've done it, you will be more likely to recognize these things as hindrances in your walk with God. You will want to take each issue to God, removing these obstacles from your life as soon as possible.

Here are some of the enemies and roadblocks to answered prayer:

- Unforgiveness (Matthew 5:24)

- Hatred (Matthew 5:24)

- Doubt (Matthew 17:41; 21:21 Mark 9:14-29)

- Fear (Matthew 14:30)

- Unconfessed sin (Isaiah 59:2)

Now I will show you how to begin your path to freedom from the burden of unforgiveness.

Steps to Freedom

1. **Confess.** After you examine yourself,
   ask God to forgive and cleanse you:

   *If we confess our sins, He is faithful and
   just to forgive us our sins and to cleanse
   us from all unrighteousness.* 1 John 1:9

2. **Accept forgiveness and cleans-
   ing.**
   Walk in faith with a conscience void
   of offense toward God.

   *Let us draw near with a true heart in full
   assurance of faith, having our hearts
   sprinkled from an evil conscience and our
   bodies washed with pure water.* Hebrews
   10:22

Noted University Study
Below is an excerpt from *Stanford Medicine*,
Volume 16, Number 4, Summer 1999, which
is published quarterly by Stanford University
Medical Center:

The Art and Science of Forgiveness

If you feel good but want to feel even better, try forgiving someone.
—*FREDERIC LUSKIN, PH.D.*

For centuries, the world's religious and spiritual traditions have recommended the use of forgiveness as a balm for hurt or angry feelings. Psychotherapists have worked to help their clients to forgive, and some have written about the importance of forgiveness. Until recently, however, the scientific literature has not had much to say about the effect of forgiveness. But that's starting to change. While the scientific study of forgiveness is just beginning—the relevant intervention research having been conducted only during the past ten years—when taken together, the work so far demonstrates the power of forgiveness to heal emotional wounds and hints that forgiveness may play a role in physical healing as well.

What is intriguing about this research is that even people who are not depressed or particularly anxious can obtain the improved emotional and psychological functioning that comes from learning to forgive. This suggests that forgiveness may enable people who are functioning adequately to feel even better. Published studies on forgiveness have shown the importance of forgiveness training on coping with a variety of psychologically painful experiences. Studies have been conducted with adolescents who felt neglected by their parents, with women who were abused as children, with elderly women who felt hurt or uncared for, with males who disagreed with their female partners' decisions to have abortions and with college students who had been hurt. These studies showed that when given forgiveness training of varying lengths and intensities, participants could become less hurt and become more able to forgive their offenders.

Receiving Forgiveness

Forgiving others is powerful, according to the above study, and it brings emotional and physical benefits to your life. It also can benefit the lives of those being forgiven. Perhaps there can now be the opportunity for healing in a once severed relationship.

Forgiveness gives us a clear conscience and the associated peace of mind that it brings. "Forgive, and be forgiven" is good advice.

Let your requests be made known to God; and the peace of God, which surpasses all understanding, will guard your hearts and minds through Christ Jesus. Philippians 4:6–7

A Prayer Workshop to Get Started!

1. Confess and receive forgiveness for any sin, including unforgiveness, doubt, unbelief, fear, and anything else that might be between you and God
(1 John 1:9).

2. List your requests. "...Let your requests be made known to God"
(Philippians 4:6).

3. Take authority over the enemy. Pray that God will "overthrow and overturn the works of darkness"
(2 Chronicles 25:8).

4. Pray in detail. Make specific (scriptural) requests to the Father in Jesus' name. You can always add "If it be Your will" on the end of a prayer if you don't know the will of God.

5. Place your trust in His specific promises. Know that it is faith in Who God is, in

His integrity, and in the integrity of His Word in which we rest our faith.

6. Thank God and praise Him for what He *is doing according to His will* "...by prayer and supplication with thanksgiving, let your requests be made known to God" (Philippians 4:6).

What Is GOD'S Part?

God is faithful. His promises are true (1 Corinthians 1:20). His Word is true (Romans 3:4). He will watch over His Word to perform it (Isaiah 55:11). So, when you find promises upon which to rest your faith, God is pleased. He will hear and answer you. You must realize that God has more love and understanding for His creation than we can possibly comprehend. He is also more power-ful than we can grasp.

Remember

• There is joy in knowing that God is alive and well and that He is interested in you!

He wants to answer your prayers. Did you know that in two of the gospels it says, "Everyone who asks receives" (Matthew 7:8, Luke 11:10)?

- Jesus said to ask and we would receive that our joy be full (John 16:23–24).

CHAPTER SEVENTEEN

Prayer Promises

TO REST YOUR FAITH UPON

Included in this chapter are some promises of God that you can trust in and rest your faith in when you pray. I have also included other Scripture that has brought great comfort to my heart. I hope the verses will bless you as well. My advice is to get a Promises of God booklet (in Christian bookstores). There are approximately seven thousand! It is inspiring to see all that belongs to us as Christians! Now for a last bit of advice...

Keep Your Mind on God

Keeping your mind on Jesus and praying about everything will bring great victory. Too much emphasis has been placed on the devil, though it is still important to address this area. Be aware; be vigilant; be vigilant in prayer.

Remember Who has the power: God does! He is limitless in power and might. Jesus is the big guy. The enemy is defeated.

The prayer method in this book works.

In the garden of Gethsemane Jesus said that He could pray to His Father and the Father would send Him legions of angels (Matthew 26:53). Pray to the Father in Jesus' name, and ask for Him to send His holy angels to fight for you, rescue you or a friend, etc.

Even though Jesus made it so simple, that in no way diminishes the limitless power of God moving on your behalf when you pray to the Father in Jesus' name, rest in Him and His Word, and thank Him for what He is doing and will do.

The simple promise of God to respond when we ask in Jesus' name is profound. The promises of God have His limitless power to back them.

The answer comes when you pray in line with God's Word. You will get results when you follow the scriptural principles.

The Promises Are Yours

The Bible tells that all provisions, or promises contained in His Word belong to you. "Then Peter opened his mouth and said, 'In truth I perceive that God shows no partiality' " (Acts 10:34). What He gave to Christians in the Bible, He gives to all Christians today.

We know that through the New Birth we are indwelt by the Holy Spirit. The Holy Spirit IS His divine nature. Think about that! Scripture says that we are partakers of His divine nature!

As His divine power has given to us all things that pertain to life and godliness, through the knowledge of Him who called us by glory and virtue, by which have been given to us exceedingly great and precious promises, that through these you may be partakers of the divine nature, having escaped the corruption that is in the world through lust. 2 Peter 1:3-4

If you abide in Me, and My words abide in you, you will ask what you desire, and it shall be done for you. John 15:7

This Book of the Law shall not depart from your mouth, but you shall meditate in it day and night, that you may observe to do according to all that is written in it. For then you will make your way prosperous, and then you will have good success. Joshua 1:8

For this reason we also thank God without ceasing, because when you received the word of God which you heard from us, you welcomed it NOT as the word of men, but as it is in truth, the word of God, which also effectually works in you who believe. 1 Thessalonians 2:13

It is the Spirit who gives life; the flesh profits nothing. The words that I speak to you are spirit, and they are life. John 6:63

So shall My Word be that goes forth from My mouth; it shall not return to Me void, but it shall accomplish what I please, and it shall prosper in the thing for which I sent it. Isaiah 55:11

And what is the exceeding greatness of His power toward us who believe, according to the working of His mighty power which He worked in Christ when He raised Him from the dead...
Ephesians 1:19–20

For we are His workmanship, created in Christ Jesus for good works, which God prepared beforehand that we should walk in them. Ephesians 2:10

In Time of Trouble

He who has begun a good work in you will complete it until the day of Jesus Christ. Philippians 1:6

*And the Lord will deliver me from every
evil work and preserve me for His
heavenly kingdom. To Him be glory
forever and ever. Amen!* 2 Timothy 4:18

For Protection

*No evil shall befall you, nor shall any
plague come near your dwelling; for He
shall give His angels charge over you, to
keep you in all your ways.*
Psalm 91:10–11

Promises for Answered Prayer

*Be anxious for nothing, but in everything
by prayer and supplication, with thanksgiving, let your requests be made known
to God and the peace of God, which
surpasses all understanding, will guard
your hearts and minds through Christ
Jesus.* Philippians 4:6-7

*And whatever you ask in My name, that I
will do, that the Father may be glorified*

in the Son. If you ask anything in My name, I will do it. John 14:13–14

And in that day you will ask Me nothing. Most assuredly, I say to you, whatever you ask the Father in My name He will give you. Until now you have asked nothing in My name. Ask, and you will receive, that your joy may be full. John 16:23–24

For all the promises of God in Him are Yes, and in Him Amen, to the glory of God through us. 2 Corinthians 1:20

Now to Him who is able to do exceedingly abundantly above all that we ask or think, according to the power that works in us, to Him be glory in the church by Christ Jesus to all generations, forever and ever. Amen. Ephesians 3:20–21

And my God shall supply all your need according to His riches in glory by Christ Jesus. Philippians 4:19

Now this is the confidence that we have in Him, that if we ask anything according to His will, He hears us. And if we know that He hears us, whatever we ask, we know that we have the petitions that we have asked of Him. 1 John 5:14–15

Therefore humble yourselves under the mighty hand of God, that He may exalt you in due time, casting all your care upon Him, for He cares for you.
1 Peter 5:6–7

Jesus' Words

And when you pray, you shall not be like the hypocrites. For they love to pray standing in the synagogues and on the corners of the streets, that they may be seen by men. Assuredly, I say to you, they have their reward. But you, when you pray, go into your room, and when you have shut your door, pray to your Father who is in the secret place; and your Father who sees in secret will reward you openly. And when you pray, do not use vain repetitions as the heathen do. For they think that they will be heard for their many words. Therefore do not be like them. For your Father knows the things you have need of before you ask Him. In this manner, therefore, pray:

Our Father in heaven, hallowed be Your name. Your kingdom come. Your will be done on earth as it is in heaven. Give us this day our daily bread. And forgive us our debts, as we forgive our debtors. And do not lead us into temptation, but deliver us from the evil one. For Yours is the kingdom and the power and the glory forever. Amen.

For if you forgive men their trespasses, your heavenly Father will also forgive you. But if you do not forgive men their trespasses, neither will your Father forgive your trespasses. Matthew 6:5–15

Part Three

Prayer Journal

Today's Date_____

My Prayers...

_____

_____

_____

_____

_____

_____

_____

_____

_____

_____

_____

_____

_____

Today's Date_____

My Answers...

_____

_____

_____

_____

_____

_____

_____

_____

_____

_____

_____

_____

_____

_____

My Thoughts...

_____

_____

_____

_____

_____

_____

_____

_____

_____

_____

_____

_____

_____

_____

*Today's Date*_____

My Prayers...

_____

_____

_____

_____

_____

_____

_____

_____

_____

_____

_____

_____

_____

Today's Date_____

My Answers...

_____

_____

_____

_____

_____

_____

_____

_____

_____

_____

_____

_____

_____

_____

My Thoughts...

_____

_____

_____

_____

_____

_____

_____

_____

_____

_____

_____

_____

_____

*Today's Date*_____

My Prayers...

_____

_____

_____

_____

_____

_____

_____

_____

_____

_____

_____

_____

_____

*Today's Date*_____

My Answers...

_____

_____

_____

_____

_____

_____

_____

_____

_____

_____

_____

_____

_____

My Thoughts...

_____

_____

_____

_____

_____

_____

_____

_____

_____

_____

_____

_____

_____

*Today's Date*_____

My Prayers...

_____

_____

_____

_____

_____

_____

_____

_____

_____

_____

_____

_____

_____

Today's Date_____

My Answers...

_____

_____

_____

_____

_____

_____

_____

_____

_____

_____

_____

_____

_____

_____

_____

My Thoughts...

_____

_____

_____

_____

_____

_____

_____

_____

_____

_____

_____

_____

_____

*Today's Date*_____

My Prayers...

_____

_____

_____

_____

_____

_____

_____

_____

_____

_____

_____

_____

_____

*Today's Date*_____

My Answers...

_____

_____

_____

_____

_____

_____

_____

_____

_____

_____

_____

_____

_____

_____

_____

My Thoughts...

_____

_____

_____

_____

_____

_____

_____

_____

_____

_____

_____

_____

_____

*Today's Date*_____

My Prayers...

_____

_____

_____

_____

_____

_____

_____

_____

_____

_____

_____

_____

_____

*Today's Date*_____

My Answers...

_____

_____

_____

_____

_____

_____

_____

_____

_____

_____

_____

_____

_____

My Thoughts...

_____

_____

_____

_____

_____

_____

_____

_____

_____

_____

_____

_____

_____

*Today's Date*_____

My Prayers...

_____

_____

_____

_____

_____

_____

_____

_____

_____

_____

_____

_____

_____

_____

Today's Date_____

My Answers...

_____

_____

_____

_____

_____

_____

_____

_____

_____

_____

_____

_____

My Thoughts...

_____

_____

_____

_____

_____

_____

_____

_____

_____

_____

_____

_____

_____

Today's Date_____

My Prayers...

_____

_____

_____

_____

_____

_____

_____

_____

_____

_____

_____

_____

Today's Date_____

My Answers...

_____

_____

_____

_____

_____

_____

_____

_____

_____

_____

_____

_____

_____

My Thoughts...

_____

_____

_____

_____

_____

_____

_____

_____

_____

_____

_____

_____

_____

*Today's Date*_____

My Prayers...

_____

_____

_____

_____

_____

_____

_____

_____

_____

_____

_____

_____

_____

*Today's Date*_____

My Answers...

_____

_____

_____

_____

_____

_____

_____

_____

_____

_____

_____

_____

My Thoughts...

_____

_____

_____

_____

_____

_____

_____

_____

_____

_____

_____

_____

_____

_____

*Today's Date*_____

My Prayers...

_____

_____

_____

_____

_____

_____

_____

_____

_____

_____

_____

_____

_____

_____

*Today's Date*_____

My Answers...

_____
_____
_____
_____
_____
_____
_____
_____
_____
_____
_____
_____
_____
_____

~ NOTES ~

~ NOTES ~